THE

LYRICAL TALES OF

A SURVIVOR

Aziza Robertson

Copyright

Table of Contents

Rebellious

Well, here we go again. Cut deep, shut down;

sewed up, discipled, and nursed back to win.

Move further in your calling,

or back down and keep your deathly living.

For death in Christ is to gain.

So, why are you breathing?

No time for worrying about how people view

you.

The way the world views you, at any rate, is not

in love, and it won't come with a godly rebuke.

So why allow something that didn't create you

to dictate your every move?

This world was made for you to walk through,
not pop a squat, kick back your feet, set up
camp, and allow the devil to make room.
Stop trying to be where God doesn't want you;
It's not worth the life you will have in the
eternal.

Breakthrough.
It's Me you want, so stop playing yourself.

How about you just let Me make do?
I guarantee it's better than whatever the enemy
has set up for you.

Go ahead, you can keep rebelling. It's really not
your choice anyway. I love you and I'm jealous
for you.
So, good luck running.

Tied

I can see you, looking at me like you do.

Like what you see? Well, I'm not the Truth.

I will use you;

pull at your heartstrings; get you into me.

So stuck that you can't see how I'm about to

make you bleed.

Let me see.

What can I use, or maybe who?

Your mother, your father, your friend from up

the street, your issues, your job, your teacher, or

maybe that new boo you accrued from the club

last week.

Now you're weak.

Now with my hooks, I can sink

deep into you, latch on, so that it becomes what

you feel to be,

a natural part of you.

So that when you move, it does too.

Oh, you thought the Holy Spirit was moving

you?

Thought you were on track, too? That was your

emotions, boo. See, this is what soul-ties do;

I like to create smoke screens and facades,

and I'm glad to use them on you. Now you

cannot do, in God,

what you're supposed to do.

I thought you knew, I'm classic with my

holdbacks.

Stagnation is the first thing on my menu.

You can fight me, but you and I both know you

don't want to, obviously, since you refuse to let

go of those things that are so close, but are yet

killing you.

Makes my job easier anyways. So, keep acting
like you know God; keep acting like you're
really in-tune.
Even I know, true repentance is the only thing
that will deliver you.
But I'm not worried, You don't even want to
know the truth, because you're stuck in your
ways,
stuck on staying up on game, stuck on making
sure you fit in your group,
stuck, because my lies feel so good and
comfortable to you. So, stay comfortable in
yourself, and know that I will stay tied to you.
Don't worry, I'll keep your swag on point for
you; make sure you live life how you want to.
Death will come quickly, too, because I have a
little place just for you.

Sanity in Ink

I once heard a writer say that this is what keeps
him sane: Paper and ink.
See, I also thought that was me.
However, I discovered that there was a missing
link; It's the God in me that keeps my sanity,
That is expressed by words in ink.

Deciphering reality from "fictionality," This
world has thrown me for a loop.
A few stories in this piece; Begin with lies and
end in truth.

I have to strive for the mark, and that too?
Really not an easy task to execute.

But I know the victory You've already produced,
So please, encourage me, while I attempt to
encourage you.

So, imagine if you will, living a lie. You're
confronted with the truth, and absentmindedly,
you reply, "God, this can't be you."
See, you're not a God of confusion, and I don't
appreciate this intrusion on the marathon I was
winning, only to find out that I'm really losing.

My mental stability is fading away. My clarity is
becoming a gray haze.
This is nothing like anything I've learned in my
past; This contradictory mess made all of those
lessons shatter, like glass.
Like going from reality to the Matrix, in a flash.
Like you know, Morpheus gave you the wrong
pill, so you're trying to regurgitate it, and fast.

What?

You never thought a white lie could make your
world crash?

Deciphering reality from "fictionality," This
world has thrown me for a loop.

A few stories in this piece; Begin with lies and
end in truth.

I have to strive for the mark, and that too?

Really not an easy task to execute.

But I know the victory You've already produced,

So please, encourage me, while I attempt to
encourage you.

So maybe the issue is not the untelling of the
truth; Maybe it's the separation of the real and
fake with you.

There's always a method to the madness when
people do what they do,

But you can't figure out why they were in your
face when they knew they couldn't stand you.

Now, maybe you're hearing incorrectly, but did
they really just say, "I love you,"
Knowing full well, they're the source of the
rumor about who you gave VD to.
Or maybe it's the hypo-gospel you've been
exposed to.

Preachers twist up God's Word, and have the
congregation following suit. From, "For God so
loved the world," to, "He won't love you unless
this amount in tithes you produce."
And since reading the Word is only a Sunday
thing for you, the preacher has you screwed up
in the head too.

It could be a life and death situation for you.

"It's okay, boo, I'm cool," is all you can
remember him saying to you.
And he definitely had you fooled. Especially
when the doctor says,
"With that recently transmitted HIV flowing
through your veins, I'd consider your now ex-
husband to be rather cruel."
Now death comes quickly to you,
and all you can think of is whether your life was
worth the absence of truth.

I once heard a writer say that this is what keeps
him sane: Paper and ink.
See, I also thought that was me.
However, I discovered that there was a missing
link:

God said the truth shall set you free, and that
where His Spirit is, there is liberty.

Through the lies, it's the God in me that has kept my sanity, which is expressed by words in ink.

The End of Me

I knew I was going to mess this up.

I tried and failed; now I feel like giving up.

God, I did what You told me to do, but I'm

feeling like,

Jesus, why didn't you come through?

This is over, and I wasn't even in the wrong. See,

I did the job he was supposed to do; Yet he got

mad when his ego suffered too.

There's got to be more to life than what I just

went through, leaving me with a view of God

that has to be misconstrued.

God, this was supposed to be my destiny... I'm

crying out, but I doubt you're hearing me.

"My child, you have your beginning, confused
with your ending.

See, where you think it ends, is really where I
begin.

And, what you think is broken, is 'spiritually-
speaking,' Already passed the 'mend,' And into
the 'sins-forgotten.'

See, there's no bad timing with Me.

I have your future laid out, complete with tests,
storms, and victories,

Only to make you stronger,

so that you can fulfill your destiny.

Blessings beyond your imagination is what I aim
for, you see.

Half-stepping, I cannot; I've pulled out all the
stops, because you belong to Me.

Now, why would I stop now?

When there's such a calling on you, for Me?

My child, you already know that is not my style.

My style is for you to come to me as a child. A

baby, with total and complete trust in Me.

For only then will you see,

That your 'end' is really My Beginning."

What I See

See, I've never been a writer,

But here I am, spitting to you the words from my

pen and pad,

With God's voice in my ears, speaking truth,

this is what I present to you.

Applaud if you want to,

but it's not me whom you should give the praise

to.

Though it would be lovely for you to uplift me,

because of my empowering you, I won't take

credit for the phrases of wisdom and truth that

God used me to speak to you.

I'm sitting and thinking, writing in a few
different locations, to get my creative juices
flowing.

I'm thinking about what to write and how I'm
feeling. I could continue to talk about my
extreme dislike.

For the terms and actions subcategorized under
the verb "write." But since I'd be using that very
vehicle as an outlet for my feelings, this poem
would be one of irony, with a hint of boredom,

leaving me with a few things unexpressed.
Since that's the case, I've decided to write about
what I see spiritually.

Now, on a spiritual tip, some of these leaders in
church must think they have God's people
tricked.

Now that is my blunt opinion, so in love,

I just don't agree with how some of them
perform, I mean, minister at their churches.

How is it that a person is a pastor,

And they don't have the discernment to know

when the Holy Spirit is present, how it operates,

nor how it looks when it's manifested in one of

your saints?

Collectively, we as Christians are coming off as

weak.

Or maybe we've been babied so long,

We don't realize it, nor do we know any other

way to be.

Milk or solid food; which one do you eat? Steak-

eater, or spiritual similac-drinker; Which one do

you want to be?

Oh, excuse me if I'm exposing people,

That's just God using me.

And believe me, this exposition didn't come short for me.

I struggle too, sometimes thinking the world revolves around me: "Forget about you, I'm going through *this*. Everyone needs to pray for me."

I Need Help.

NO, I don't get down and pray on my knees;

Girl, this dress is Versace!

Cry out to God?

Yeah, while it's extra loud and the church is rocking, and only on row three, so that the pastor is sure to notice me.

And, when I've shown enough of my face so

everyone knows I'm a faithful member of this
illustrious church, I put my finger up and leave,
because Pastor always puts me to sleep
whenever he starts to preach."

This might not be you, but brothers and sisters,
we have to do better.
This goes out to the young and the seasoned;
Have we forgotten what it is we were created
for?

God's grace and mercy endures forever. Our
bodies don't.

We are all accountable for doing what was made
known to us when we get up there.
So, how do you know the entire Bible, but
putting it into action is what you don't?
Don't even use the excuse of, "That's my

struggle; God knows my heart."

Your heart is deceitfully wicked,

And you can't be too lazy to do your part. No,

I'm not judging, and if you see differently, then

feel free to judge me,

and please excuse my way of thinking, if you feel

the need.

My past is something that I'm not proud of, but

from that, I'm growing.

So obviously, a "holier-than-thou" role is not one

for which I'm aiming. Disappointment in how

some of us are treating God and His people is

the more explanatory feeling.

See, I've never been a writer,

But here I am, spitting to you the words from my

pen and pad, with God's voice in my ears,

speaking truth; from that, is what I present to

you.

Applaud if you want to, but it's not me to whom you should give the praise. Though it would be lovely for you to uplift me, because of my empowering you, I won't take credit for the phrases of wisdom and truth that God used me to speak to you.

One in the Same

Trust and love are beginning to be synonymous.

As I raise my eyes to Heaven,

God, this is Your promise: Never leave me nor

forsake me; Your thoughts and actions towards

me, I revere greatly.

Lord. You. Are.

My Love, my Source, my Peace; My Comfort,

My Protector, My Being.

I owe You my life; so much I've found in You.

Now, with this relationship, I declare my trust in

You.

Why?

Because You love me, and showed me what love
can be.

So, in turn, I declare my love for You.

This. Is. True.

I don't always understand the ways You have or
the things You do.

But my character is expanding because I go and
make it through.

God, I'm on a never-ending pursuit for my life
to end; walking through those gorgeous gates,
with a "Well Done" from You.

I. Don't. Deserve.

You, Your love, or Your blessings, This life, Your
grace, or Your mercies.

I could go over my life, combing through every
strand to figure out how I gained the
opportunity to be Yours, Lord.

However, the older I get, the bigger the mistakes
I make.

Show me that I can never be that blessed solely
on the deeds that supposedly built up a part of
my worth, but rather more on the cross and sins
your Son bore.

And, speaking of worth;

I could say that I'm not worthy of Your love,
Lord, but since You love me, others will love me
too.

However, after searching deeper in Him and
finding me, on the contrary,

others don't have to love me or like me.

They can't because they lack the ability.

Talk about a different view.

I'm a commodity, not a rag doll or doormat you
can step onto.

God's love is beyond me and you,

So why put up with someone who will walk all

over you, and have no Heaven, only hell, to put

you through?

God calls us to love as He loves.

Is that what your friendships and other

relationships are doing for you?

Better yet, are you?

Or is the meaning of true love and counterfeit

love, one and the same to you?

The Warning

I'm waiting for you, but I'm not an order taker,

especially when money, clothes, shoes, and new

"boo's," remain on your list of things for Me to

have favor.

Is My Kingdom the first thing you seek, or the

last stop before you go off and do you,

completely?

I'm in love with you, but I'm not a doormat for

you to walk over or walk to; decide it's cute, but

not for you.

Then proceed to do what you got to do.

Oh, that's not you? Ms. "He-knows-my-heart-

and-deep

-down-inside-I'm-saved-and-sanctified-too!"
Your words are not lining up at all with your
fruits.

I am the Giver of Life
and the Creator of all that surrounds you, but I
will not be used.
My, my, aren't we so selfish…
And yet you wonder why people can't see Me
through you.

It takes a Holy magnifying glass to see if you are
really in-tune, yet even then, the view is
misconstrued.
I know you know Me, but sweetie, who are you?
There's no relationship here, only a list of wants,
not needs, and a worrying spirit when it's those
very things I choose not to meet.
You must see.

I Am the Lord of all, not your personal Santa.

Once or twice a year, you come to My house, dressed in your best, offering up phony, showy praise, acting like you know Me better than the rest.

You're a hot mess.

I don't know you or your fruits because you've never given me your best.

You haven't passed any of my tests,

And as of right now, you have no life after death;
Only pain beyond your imagination, with no hint of rest.

And don't say I didn't warn you. You insisted on wanting the best.

It's a shame you only wanted it during this life,

instead of also after death.

Oh, and that's not just the burying of the flesh. It
is also your desires lining up with Mine,

your will conforming to My Will for you.

That's what I'm referring to.

You can truly live for me by dying and taking
up the cross I bared for you.

Or, you may continue to feel free living how you
do.

Just know, when you have to answer to Me, at
the end of all this, I can only say, "Depart from
Me, I never knew you."

Interlude (part 1)

Heart shift, Mind follows.

Spirit Lead, flesh bows.

Let My people hear the truth.

This world is dying.

You will be lost if it is not

in Christ the Savior, you take root.

Attacked

It's crazy how,

One minute, you and God are tight, and in the
next moment,

You feel spiritually "schizoid," ready to fight.

It seems like your God-high came crashing
down, and you're searching, but

He's nowhere to be found.

You become panic-stricken and you feel like
you're losing your mind, while God is patiently
sitting on the sidelines, waiting to see how your
following actions will morph with the passing
time.

See, He let the enemy step in to test your
endurance, seeing if you'll operate under a flesh,

or spiritual, influence.

Since you walk around claiming the God you
serve is real, in order to boost your maturity,
He takes you out of your comfort zone.
You stay in your word, right? The fiery darts
from the enemy are coming at you.
You have your Faith-shield for blocking, and
your Spirit-sword for fighting?
Oh yeah, I forgot.
It's not an everyday thing for you… And what
you do consume goes in one way, and out the
other, like junk food.
Does that make you a fool?

Let's be honest.
Reading and hearing are not the same as
listening and understanding.
That's the problem with some people, too.

Not you?

So your truth is that you comprehend all of
what's being told to you, via the Holy Spirit.

You're hearing the word "endurance," and
you're starting to fear it.
You've passed tests and overcome things before;
Yet you get a little upset when God says, "I
want to do more."

So then, the things you struggled with
and thought you overcame in the past, come
back; At first glance, you're okay with that.
Now, the harder-to-hurdle problems are starting
to come to a head, and out of frustration, you
bluntly say,
"I don't care what You're up to, God. This is
wack."

The issue is, you forgot that you're not by
yourself when you're under a spiritual attack.
You forgot that your Father had previously
created your spiritual comeback.
So, with His strength, you will come out of this
blessed, wiser, and stronger, with your spiritual
endurance intact.

The Lyrical Tales of a Survivor

Everybody has a song to sing. Everyone has a
story to tell.

These are the lyrical tales of a survivor.

Mental strain.

He's hitting me over and over again.

I can't take the pain.

Let an ending to his fist meeting my face and ribs
be my immediate gain.

He said it again: "Forget your life and that dumb
God you serve."

Please tell me this is a game. If I play my cards
right, will there be a quicker end? Can I pass Go,

collect $200, and start over again?

Go back to before he started sleeping around on
me with women and men, before the constant
struggles with insecurities and Chlamydia, both
of which he blamed me for getting.

Even farther back to before I met him, when my
life meant something more than the wooden
broom he wakes me up with in the morning.

That, and the swift kick to my side to get me
going. All of these bruises signify the love he's
showing me.

But with God's strength, I'm picking up my hurt
body and leaving, blindly going, with faith
being the only thing on which I'm running.
Physically, I'm choosing life and eternal living.

Physical abuse isn't the only situation in which
survival is commended.

Financial punching and slapping

have become an economic reality that seems

never-ending.

More than enough for some to suffer from

suicidal tendencies… no one ever said life was

easy.

It's more like facing first-day cases as a beginner

social worker, which is what it could be; Things

being seen way beyond your wildest yet most

sickening dreams.

Yes, financial burdens can seem and be just that

cruel and mean.

Yet, God calls us to face these things; a battle felt

but unseen.

It's a faith fight; God's thing.

Lyrics to the songs and lines to the tales of

survivors like you and me.

Thriving? I'm trying.

Sickness is felt by every human being.

Whether it is physical, emotional, spiritual, or
mental, I'm dying.

Like keeping someone bound by chains, I'm
fighting to push past the pain and anguish I
wake up with every morning.

God, I'm trying.

Seeking and hoping to soon find the Banner,
Comforter, Healer, Protector, and Provider in
Him, but I'm still not finding.

All of this negativity brought on by the enemy.

He's giving ME the power to start binding;

I'm binding…There's my Savior!

The devil is a liar.

I feel my Help coming, I'm SURVIVING.

If it weren't for God's Kingdom that I would
gain;

If there were no testimony of victory after the
pain;

If there were no sunshine after the storm and
rain;

If I went through hell and high water just to
come out the same, every second, of every
minute, of my living would be in vain.

The repeated results of others' lives being
shamed. That cycle has to change.

We are more than conquerors in Jesus' Name.

Winning this battle is worth the pain. These are
the lyrical tales of a survivor,

With everlasting peace and victory as their gain.

Truth

The Word is as sharp as a double-edged sword.

Okay, we know that rebellion is not acceptable

in His Kingdom.

So stop sleeping on it and utilize its power some

more.

You are poured into and fed a buffet of scripture

and experience much impartation.

Yet your life has yet to show any signs of

manifestation.

God is patient, but He won't wait that long.

Yes, His grace is sufficient, so get up and move

on. You're slacking where you should be

packing, getting ready to get some souls won.

But, of course, you're stuck on you; Waiting on

what God has already told you to do.

About your overly-analyzed and conjured-up situation, and yet you still feel the need to hold up, on the building up, of God's nation.

Because, after all, it's all about what you do for the Kingdom; all about what He called you to do, and you must take your time to make sure you don't over-exert yourself, because so much is required of you, since you are chosen, predestined, pre-ordained, designated before birth, the only one who can save, since God only gave that power to you...you, you, you, you...

Wait.

Stop before you get rebuked. Oh, you say that's not true?
Well, since His Kingdom supposedly revolves around you, I figured you'd just go ahead,

And do this without His help,

Since it's all about you.

See, the children of Israel had the truth twisted
too: Rebellious, complaining about their
situation, refused to operate in their proper
position, and steadily insisting on not truly
following the "inconvenience" of God's rules;

A lot of frustration and anguish ensued.

Forty years to do a 3-day journey, steadily
clinging to the past, never letting go of old
habits, and remaining in denial of the truth, had
them re-walking the same route.

Now, don't tell me that's not a spiritual mirror of
you.

The same tests over and over again got you
upset.

You can't get mad;

You don't have a Kingdom mindset.

You want to keep the peace.

Jesus came to separate the goats from the sheep;

It's in His Word.

And you're steadily trying to make sure People's

feelings don't get hurt.

Your submission to Christ is the standard.

Go ahead and pout; The truth just came out.

And don't go and get upset, just because it's

your mindset

That God has chosen to address. Don't you

know God gives you a word, and you must walk

it out, not shut down all communication and do

nothing for the Kingdom

Until you have fixed your wounded pride and

finally decide to come out.

You don't have to throw a fit,

Just because the world you built up got hit.

Take it to God, with a repenting spirit.

Let Him know you messed up, and you need

His forgiveness. Trust He will forgive and forget,

get you back on course,

Like nothing ever happened.

But don't abuse it, because then you'll lose it.

The enemy's crouching at your door,

Ready for you to slack off on your Christ-walk

movement.

I pray you receive this, and take heed,

Because this is where the truth is.

A Picture of Authority

I had a dream during prayer one night; More
like a vision, is what it seemed.

So unnaturally, it happened at the end of a Bible
study. So off---because it wasn't during my
personal time.

It happened amongst my people, my peers, my
kind.

God said, "It's revelation time. I'm going to
show you what I see and prove to you that
things are not as they seem.

I'm going to paint for you, a picture, of
authority.

I see people strategically placed.

Don't know the specific place, but I am shown a

specific face.

Funny, because that person was just at my place

yesterday, supposedly coming by, just to say

"Hey!"

I then immediately realize I am unknowingly

doing what I am supposed to; I'm keeping my

friends close and my enemies closer.

But God said, "That wasn't all of what I'm

showing you."

God, I don't get it…Weren't You showing me

that person and their plans, so that when they

strike, I have the upper hand?

He said, "Yes, but you got the wrong man." He

said, "Take a closer look." So, a deeper insight

into a picture that He painted is what I took.

I noticed that there were about 30 other people

in front of me, yelling, telling me what I am

And what I will always be.

I asked God, Why is it this that you are showing

me?

These were supposed to be friends and family

that I love.

In reply, He said, "Let me show my peripheral

vision from my standpoint above."

I said, "Okay, God, but wait..." Too late.

He said nothing as He showed me the linear

diamond shape, which the thirty-plus people

were standing in.

He showed me the devil, standing just outside

of it, with a smug look of supposed innocence.

He was speaking black air onto them.

God showed me their backs turned to Him,

So that when they spoke, they didn't even know

it was them that the enemy was usin'.

God said, "Don't get mad at the people with
their nay-saying; I just showed you that Satan is
lazy. Those people regurgitating negativity at
your life and your being---

That's their response to the enemy feeding them
blasphemy, trying to get back at Me.

This is your picture of authority.

He put me back in my place and took the people
off mute.

I look up to God, and in the back of my head, I
know the devil must think his actions are cute.

My Abba already told me what to do,

So, in response to the negativity, it's God's Word
I spewed.

God whispered in my ear, "I like the view," and
He immediately showed me the reactions to the

words He gave me to spew.

Black air pushed out by white, with the enemy
in the back looking extremely confused.

God said, "That's what happens when you
operate in the truth. Now go and walk in the
picture of authority that I painted for you."

Warrior

Warrior, warrior, get in line; it's time.

Align yourself in the battle of the spirits and
principalities,

On Jesus' side, where you will serve gladly.

You have been uprooted from those things that
are not of Christ.

Now, fight.

The spirit of the Anti-Christ is running rapidly,

tearing down unity, faith, peace, and

selflessness, and building up strongholds.

Take hold.

Get your sword and shield; The carnal mind

can't win on this spiritual battlefield.

To the Sword of the Spirit, and the Shield of
Faith, the devil must yield.

I hope you weren't looking for an easy path,
with a comfortable feel.

Warrior, that's just not real. Know that fear has
no room,

Shame has been shown the door, and insecurities
have no place in the pockets of your armor.

Stand up, Warrior.

There is much work to be done.

Can't stop; won't stop, not until the war is won.

The Barter (Interlude, Part 2)

Separated by life, connected by death, brought
the miracle of peace,
And the birth of rest. Life in abundance,
Because of the sacrifice of flesh. This is the price
of salvation.
A Barter, met.

A Holy thrown, for a carpenter's bag.
Worshipping and praising, for a deadly walk
with a cross, and the luxury of being spat at.
To give us an example of how to live, so that we
may get to the promised land.
A sacrifice met, with all power in His hands.

Trust

So, God has me on this "trust" thing.

Like life wasn't hard enough, NOW, He wants
me to trust Him.

I say, "Nope, Pops, I can do this on my own,"
while I continue running in circles, trying to
figure out where I went wrong.

It's nothing big; I just have to figure out why
this went that way, and why that went this
way… And why this and that went those
ways…

And, why does my heart say to go God's way
and have Him save the day?

But God, trust isn't easy.

I trust someone to do this, then they don't come
through, then I struggle to complete it, then they
come back after it's all said and done, and yet
you still expect me to trust you?
I don't think what you're saying is completely
true.

I could hear Him say, "Why can't you see that
man is not Me?
See, unlike man, I come through; unlike you, I
do better than you can do for you.
My repertoire is extensive, and yes, the cost of
your time may be expensive, but in time, you'll
see that trusting in Me is all you need.
My Word does not and cannot return void;
don't you see the eternal warranty?

I can be more than your imagination can conjure
up, if you let Me.

My love for you is indescribable, unexplainable,
and physically unattainable; More than this cold
world will ever be.

So, trust Me."

But God, You've already done enough for me. I
got myself into this mess, so see, You don't have
to help me.

"I know all of these things, but I need you to do
something for Me. You gave Me that house you
don't live in, the car you've never driven,

That husband you haven't met yet, and those
children you haven't birthed yet, but you
haven't given Me:

That job you can't seem to get, the issues you
still regret;

The pain you can't hide, and the reasons why, to
sleep at night, you cry.

I want all of that too.

You can call it an awkward greed; I call it jealousy, because these gods are coming before Me.

I know you don't really expect you to get yourself completely through. So, trust Me and see that I've always been all you'll ever need."

Try ME

Now we've come back to this, I see.

It's been three years, and yet you still don't
completely trust Me, Daughter. How can this
be?

God, I gave you those things you told me to. I'm
not worried about my job anymore.

Yes, I know, but what about those finances of
yours?

Yes, I know God, I gave you that big debt…

But what about your car note and your rent?

But God, that money is easier to get. Just let me

figure it out, and don't worry about it.

Really? Then why haven't you paid it yet?

I want all of you, not some of you;

What kind of relationship do you think this is?

God, you know I love You.

This is a marriage, and trust Me, My love and

your love are two very different things; and

don't think you can play Me.

You're either hot or cold; Lukewarmness is not

acceptable.

Um, God, it's just a few bills.

And it's about to mess up your eternal dwelling

place in the Heavenly Hills.

Look, God, it's not that big a deal…

Did you not want Me to line up your life with
My Will?

Remember, I'm the Beginning and the End; I'm
Jehovah Jireh.

You must've forgotten who I AM; here's a
reminder. I'm the reason why you wake up in
the morning, blink your eyes, and continue to
breathe as you get up and walk around on the
legs I told to work, in the house where I blessed
you to be.

And that's hardly anything;

Don't you see you literally can't live without Me?

I can shut you down with a wink.

Yet I choose to love you in your fragility.

God, I'm…I'm sorry.

Repent, and it's all good with Me.

I'll take those smaller bills, and the worry and
stress that was growing, too.

Yes, I saw those things attempt to take root.

You'd allow it to overshadow my love for you,

and in this marriage, I'm only allowing you to
operate in truth.

So, to stay true, just let Me do what I do.

In the end, it will all be better for you, as long as
you keep Me in your view.

You can't take a little bit of Me and apply it to
worldly things.

Reality and spirituality together are an
impossibility. Don't you know reality is a
watered-down mimic of Me, which is also a
mirror image of the enemy.

All of that to say this clearly: Abide in Me, and
honestly reside in Me.

When the devil thinks He's slick, hide in Me.

When you're sick of being tricked, find Me, cry

to Me, don't deny Me, for where My Spirit is,

There is Liberty. So, Try Me.

Love

Love, a word that comes and goes, but few
people really know.

Do you really know?

I mean, do I even know?

Love; so simple, yet so complex.

Simply put: so God. Love is so God,

That is the very epitome of the Almighty,

Is that which is misused and misunderstood,

often lacking understanding from those who
possess it,

And don't even know it.

So again I ask, do you know?

I mean, do I even know?

God; Love.

Interchangeably meaningful: Jesus; Crucifixion.

Love through death makes life so beautiful.

Deeper than the eyes can see,

Deeper than the mind can conceive, and if you
allow it to be,

Small-minded-unbound, and limitation-free. But
that might be too hard to conceive.

Then I AM said to me, "Why not just let Me be
Me,

And show you the love that, only through My
being, will you see, Just how much it will please.

I see you as a baby, Me, cleaning you up.

I see you falling; Me, picking you up.

I see my younger sibling inheriting the Kingdom
with Me, as it is written in Romans 8 so

eloquently.

I see love past the fairytale scenario, and into a
world unbeknownst to man;

A realm of new beginnings with the Great I AM.
But see, because of my love,

I see that you still don't understand.

I see that you still want to do this thing by
yourself, and because of the love of My chosen
people,

I can only let you do that for so long. See, you
were bought with a price, making this life no
longer your own. Realize that I am the One who
can do

Exceedingly, abundantly, and above all that you
can think of.

I AM the One to seek and find; Yes, all of this
through Me.

I AM the Way, the Truth, and the Life.

And all I request of you is that you love Me, for

by loving Me you will live a life and eternity

beyond your wildest dreams."

And, as crazy as it may seem, and as unworthy

as you or I may be,

This is His love, God's love,

From Him to you and me.

You

Your being crosses color barriers, and translates

Your greatness into all languages.

Your love transcends the box of limitations,

We consistently put You in. No boundaries in

Him.

Jesus. My. Truth.

You're my Rock, my Joy, and my Peace.

I. Couldn't. Earn,

This life, Your chastening, Your protection, nor

Your Mercy.

Thank you for that.

I constantly forget that You are more than a big

God,

Living in a big Heaven, that Your ability to meet
us where we are at,

In all aspects, it makes you omnipotent,

omniscient, and omnipresent. More than I can
say for myself;

Fragile, selfish, and with many imperfections.

But oh, your greatness.

When I am weak without an ounce of fight in
me, You become my strength,

With Your grace, operating sufficiently.

No restrictions, only Your Spirit elevating me.

You don't put me in a box of limitations, yet that
is something I continue to do to You.

You don't reciprocate; I'm broken; You're Great,

So, what kind of sense does my lack of faith
make?

You are All-Powerful and Almighty, The
Beginning and the End,
Still, I tend to second-guess your promises.
His mark, I've missed.

It's not worth it.
If we're not ready for it, then Lord, please hold
it.
I refuse to knowingly mess up your plans, even
for a moment.
And I know that,
When I come into the full knowledge of you, I'll
know myself, for I'm striving to be,
a mirror image of the One who made me.

THE LYRICAL TALES OF A SURVIVOR